GUIDELINES

children's ministries

Ministries that Help Children Grow in Faith

Mary Alice Gran
General Board of Discipleship

CHILDREN'S MINISTRIES

Copyright © 2008 by Cokesbury

All rights reserved.
United Methodist churches and other official United Methodist bodies may reproduce up to 500 words from this publication, provided the following notice appears with the excerpted material: From *Children's Ministries 2009–2012*. Copyright © 2008 by Cokesbury. Used by permission.

Requests for quotations exceeding 500 words should be addressed to Permissions Office, Abingdon Press, P.O. Box 801, 201 Eighth Avenue South, Nashville, TN 37202-0801 or permissions@abingdonpress.com.

This book is printed on acid-free paper.

ISBN 978-0-687-64951-8

All Scripture quotations unless noted otherwise are from the New Revised Standard Version of the Bible, copyright 1989, Division of Christian Education of the National Council of the Churches of Christ in the United States of America. Used by permission. All rights reserved.

Scripture quotations marked NIV are taken from the Holy Bible, NEW INTERNATIONAL VERSION®. Copyright © 1973, 1978, 1984 by International Bible Society. All rights reserved throughout the world. Used by permission of International Bible Society.

Some paragraph numbers for and language in the Book of Discipline *may have changed in the 2008 revision, which was published after these Guidelines were printed. We regret any inconvenience.*

MANUFACTURED IN THE UNITED STATES OF AMERICA

Contents

Welcome 4
Welcome to Children's Ministries 6
    A Biblical Foundation
Getting Started 8
    What Is My Job?
    Basic Responsibilities for the Coordinator of Children's Ministries
    Quick-Start Tips
    The Coordinator of Children's Ministries
Keeping Our Commitments to Children 14
    The United Methodist Church
    A Personal Commitment
    The Congregation's Commitment
    Children's Ministry Profile
What Is Your Role in Keeping Children Safe? 19
Children in the Life of the Congregation 20
    Gifts Children Bring to the Church
The Organizational Structure of the Church 22
    Congregational Meeting Commitment Worksheet
    A Children's Ministries Council
Ministry for, with, and by Children 25
Ministry in the Community and the World 28
Organize and Plan for the Year 31
Weekday Ministries 33
    What Is Weekday Ministry?
    Weekday Ministry Programs
Resources 37
General Agency Contacts   **Inside Back Cover**

Welcome

You are so important to the life of the Christian church! You have consented to join with other people of faith who, through the millennia, have sustained the church by extending God's love to others.

You have been called and have committed your unique passions, gifts, and abilities to a position of leadership. This Guideline will help you understand the basic elements of that ministry within your own church and within The United Methodist Church.

Called to Spiritual Leadership

Each person is called to ministry by virtue of his or her baptism, and that ministry takes place in all aspects of daily life, in and outside the church. As a pastoral leader or leader among the laity, your ministry is not just a "job," but a spiritual endeavor. You *are* a spiritual leader now, and others will look to you for spiritual leadership. What does this mean?

First, *all* persons who follow Jesus are called to grow spiritually through the practice of various Christian habits (or "means of grace") such as prayer, Bible study, private and corporate worship, acts of service, Christian conferencing, and so on. Jesus taught his disciples practices of spiritual growth and leadership that you, as a disciple, are to share with others as they look to you to be a model and guide.

Second, it means that you always keep your eye on the main reasons for any ministry—to help others grow to a mature faith in God that moves them to action on behalf of others, especially "the least" (see Matthew 25:31-46). This is an aspect of "disciple making," which is the ultimate goal of all that we do in the church.

CULTIVATING VISION AND MISSION

As a spiritual leader, a primary function you carry is to help those you lead to see as clearly as possible what God is calling your church to be and to do. Ideally, your church council first forms this vision and then forms plans and goals for how to fulfill that vision. As a leader, you will help your team remain focused and accountable to honor the vision and goals to which the church is committed. You will help your team create and evaluate suggestions, plans, and activities against the measure: *Does this move us closer to our church's vision to bring others to God in this place and time?*

CHRISTIAN CONFERENCING

While there are appropriate and useful business-like practices that apply to church life, Christian practices distinguish the church as the church. In the United Methodist tradition, how we meet and work together is important. "Christian Conferencing" involves listening not only to each other, but also listening intently for the will of God in any given task or conversation. This makes prayer essential in the midst of "business as usual." As Christians, we are called to "speak the truth in love." This is a special way to speak in which we treat one another as if each of us were Christ among us. As a spiritual leader in your ministry area, you have the privilege and opportunity to teach and model these practices. By remembering that each of us is beloved of God and discerning the presence of God in all that the church does, every task becomes worshipful work.

THE MISSION OF THE UNITED METHODIST CHURCH

The United Methodist Church is a connectional church, which means in part that every local church is interrelated through the structure and organization of districts, conferences, jurisdictions, and central conferences in the larger "family" of the denomination. *The Book of Discipline of The United Methodist Church* describes, among other things, the ministry of all United Methodist Christians, the essence of servant ministry and leadership, how to organize and accomplish that ministry, and how our connectional structure works (see especially ¶¶125–138).

Our Church is more than a structure; it is a living organism. The *Discipline* describes our mission to proclaim the gospel and to welcome people into the body of Christ, to lead people to a commitment to God through Jesus Christ, to nurture them in Christian living by various means of grace, and to send persons into the world as agents of Jesus Christ (¶122). Thus, through you—and many other Christians—this very relational mission continues.

(For help in addition to this Guideline and the *Book of Discipline*, see "Resources" at the end of your Guideline, www.umc.org, and the other websites listed on the inside back cover.)

Welcome to Children's Ministries

Welcome to the world of ministry for, with, and by children: A world where we can see the smiles of children making new discoveries, feel the energy of children in a group setting, hear the sounds of children in song and in learning, and be nurtured by the insights of children as God is present in their lives. All of this makes for a fascinating ministry.

Remember your own childhood? Think of your first memories of the church. Was it a friendly place? Were you loved? Can you recall special persons or times at church? Where did you learn the stories of God and Jesus? If you didn't attend church as a child, what memories do you want to provide for children?

Think of your church today. Are children welcomed, loved, and cared for in safe surroundings? Are families encouraged, taught, and supported? Is there intentional outreach to children in the surrounding community? Are new children integrated into the life of the church in consistent, caring ways?

Children's Ministries was prepared to enable you as a leader of children's ministries in your congregation. Regardless of your church's size or structure, this Guideline is designed to help you focus on The United Methodist Church's commitment to ministry for, with, and by children. This Guideline contains ideas and suggestions to help you create a church where children experience God's love, feel included in the life of the congregation, and have opportunities to grow in their faith.

You are invited to discover the best design, the most caring persons, the best resources and materials, and the most fruitful programming for children's ministry so that children will flourish and grow in the light of God's love within the environment of your congregation. You are invited to ensure that your congregation includes children in a holistic ministry aimed toward making disciples of Jesus Christ.

Ministry for, with, and by children is an opportunity to work and grow in a variety of arenas. You are not expected to attempt this task alone. You are part of a team with:
- parents, grandparents, caregivers
- the pastor and church staff
- persons in your congregation who are concerned for children
- persons within the connectional United Methodist Church
- persons in the community who care about children.

A Biblical Foundation

Jesus loved children. Who has not heard the beloved story of young Jesus in the Temple speaking with the religious authorities (Luke 2:41-52) or seen at least one picture of the adult Jesus surrounded by and caring for children (based, for example, on Matthew 18:2-5)? Hebrew parents had an obligation to teach their children the Law and to bring them up to be responsible members of the community—which was also the community of faith. Children mattered then. Children matter now.

Jesus would have been familiar with the instructions from Deuteronomy to teach the faith story to children. These commands include, "Assemble the people before me [God] to hear my words so that they may learn to revere me as long as they live in the land and may teach them to their children" (4:10 NIV) or "When your children ask you in time to come, 'What is the meaning of the decrees and the statutes and the ordinances that the LORD our God has commanded you?' then you shall say to your children" the proper recitation of God's mighty acts in history (6:20-25). These injunctions are no less important today.

Children are our treasure, and we must take care of them. In a stinging parable (Matthew 7:9-11), Jesus reminds his hearers that even though we are sinful and make mistakes, we still tend to our children—and God, our parent, tends graciously to us. Children model the pureness of heart and joy inherent in the kingdom of God (Mark 10:13-16). They show us the way.

CHILDREN'S MINISTRIES 7

You are blessed with the most important resources for this ministry—your love for children and your commitment to care for children. With a continual prayer in your heart and God's ever present grace, your ministry will be a blessing to the children and families of your congregation and community. Now go forth, in the name of Jesus, to make a difference. Amen.

Getting Started
What Is My Job?

You are a key person in the children's ministries of your congregation. Your job, as a coordinator of children's ministries in your congregation, assures that children's faith is taken seriously in the life of your church. *Your primary task (like that of the whole church) is to help children on their journey as disciples of Jesus Christ.* Given that, what are the relationships and responsibilities for which you are accountable?

Children, and those who teach and care for them, are your primary responsibility. Model the love and care that Jesus manifested in his life in order to help children and children's leaders/teachers understand their role as disciples. Children are special persons of dignity and worth. Listen to their stories. Know them and call them by name. Keep them safe. Be an advocate for them. They are a valuable part of the congregation, with gifts and blessings to share. In all your actions and reactions, model God's unconditional love for children. The same is true for the adult leaders and teachers in your church. Care about them as children of God. Treasure them and teach them by example, word, and training.

Develop positive relationships with the children and their teachers and with other persons in the congregation. Your role as an advocate for the children will require you to have good working relationships with other congregational leaders and with a variety of other groups. In addition, having a good relationship with parents and knowing the environment or situation in which the children live will add a valuable dimension to your ministry. Developing good relationships will be particularly important if you are responsible for recruiting others to work with children.

Interpret and plan for the spiritual, mental, physical, emotional, social, and moral growth of children. This Guideline will help you respond to children's needs as you plan for activities and programs.

Basic Responsibilities for the Coordinator of Children's Ministries

The responsibilities of your position as coordinator of children's ministries will vary depending on the size and staffing of your church. *If you are in a church with few children,* you are probably the primary person responsible for seeing that the needs of children and youth are met. *If you are in a church with many children and youth,* you may be one of several age-level coordinators. *If there is a paid staff person responsible for children's ministry,* your job may be modified in relation to the staff person's duties.

Whatever the staffing or size of your church, you are responsible for meeting with the church council representing and advocating for children across the entire spectrum of your church's ministries. You have the responsibility of influencing policy and program decisions with the needs of the children in mind, keeping council members informed about the needs of children and the part they play in the life of the church. (There may also be other groups in your congregation's organizational system with whom you will meet, such as the nurture committee, education work area, or children's council.) Whatever the organizational structure of your particular congregation, it is your responsibility to:

- study the needs of children.
- stay in touch with others who care about children. They will help you design and implement programs, initiate ministries, and plan a calendar to best meet the needs of the children and the total church.
- keep in close communication with the children, their parents, and their teachers. This will help you understand the needs, wants, gifts, and graces of the children in your church. Share your understandings with the church council and the children's council as well as with the total congregation.
- pray intentionally for the children and their families.
- suggest experiences that may be new or innovative.
- advocate for the children. Be strong in your intent that children be a visible and viable part of the church family.
- be realistic in your requests. Being innovative means seeing what the possibilities are and being aware of and in tune with realistic expectations and abilities.
- speak up for quality leadership. Work with the persons who invite teachers and children's workers to help find the best persons for the job.
- speak up for adequate funding. Make sure your financial planners are aware of the needs of all ministries with children. Safe, clean rooms and equipment are expected. Materials to operate a program are as necessary

as Bibles, hymnals, and bulletins. Assure training opportunities for teachers and leaders.
- do everything possible to ensure that your church is a safe place for children and for the adults who work with them. *Safe Sanctuaries* (see Resources) will help you in this task.
- be acquainted with the curriculum and resource materials available from The United Methodist Church. *Forecast* (curriculum catalog) and Curric-U-Phone staff (1-800-251-8591) are valuable resources to aid in ministry planning and class curriculum (see Resources). Discover who the resource persons are in your district or conference and ask for their assistance.
- keep in touch with other leaders in the congregation who work with youth, adults, and families as well as other leaders who use your church space (scouts, 4-H). You can accomplish more as a team than alone.
- network with persons in other churches, if possible.

Quick-Start Tips

Make an appointment with the staff person responsible for ministry with children (the pastor or director of Christian education). Keep in close communication with that person throughout your tenure.

Study the ministry or mission statement of your congregation, if available. Use this as your guideline for evaluating current programs and developing new programs in children's ministry.

Gather other persons who also care about children. This may be an existing children's council or a team that you organize and begin.

Chair and guide the work of the council on children's ministries, your congregation's group of persons responsible for ministry with children.

Formulate your ideas into a yearly plan for ministry with children.

Report on the concerns of children and the plans for ministry to, with, for, and by children to the church council (or its counterpart).

Show appreciation for volunteers who give their time, energy, and abilities for the children, including a ritual of dedication for the teachers.

ADDITIONAL HINTS (FOR THE SAKE OF YOUR HEALTH AND SANITY)

1. You are only one person, so do not take on more responsibilities than you can handle. You may want a specific program so strongly that you agree to organize, lead, clean up, and report back to the church. However, if you do it all yourself then *(a)* others are not given the opportunity to be in ministry with children and *(b)* you will eventually suffer from burnout.

2. Know what your pastor, other staff, and church leaders expect of you. If what they expect and what you expect are different, talk now! If the job is not defined, then it is not possible for you to do it successfully. Define the job before you begin; adjust it as you identify new opportunities.

3. Celebrate each project as it is completed. Having a list of "to dos" for the year and marking them off as they are completed will give you a sense of a job well done.

4. Document and evaluate your activities—both successes and near-successes.

5. Discover persons with a passion for children's ministries who you can begin to train, to share, or take over your job in the future.

6. Take time off. Whether you are a volunteer or paid staff, don't become indispensable.

The Coordinator of Children's Ministries

Your job will be rewarding if you know what you are to do. Look over the following sample job description. With other responsible persons (for example, the pastor, the director of Christian education, and the chair of the nurture committee), personalize and date your job description based on your congregation, the setting, and your special gifts. A written job description is helpful whether you are a volunteer or a paid staff person.

Note: It is sometimes easier to think "we can do it all" than it is to be realistic. Think carefully about the time you can invest. Base your job description on available time and priorities for children's ministry in your congregation.

SAMPLE JOB DESCRIPTION: COORDINATOR OF CHILDREN'S MINISTRIES

Date Prepared: _____

General Responsibilities
- Represent and advocate for a ministry by, for, and with children in all aspects of congregational life.
- Be well acquainted with the age-level characteristics and needs of children in general and specifically in your neighborhood.
- Coordinate the ministry with children for your congregation.

Specific Responsibilities
- Guide the work of the children's council (if such a council exists).
- Evaluate and assess the present children's ministry program.
- Suggest and implement new possibilities for including children in ministry.
- Work with others, such as the pastor and trustees, to ensure that your church is a safe place for the children and the adults who work with and care for them.
- Serve as a member of the church council, charge or church conference, and other appropriate groups as an advocate for children.
- Recruit persons willing and gifted to serve in the area of children's ministry.
- Offer regular training opportunities for volunteers.
- Know available resources for children and for leaders and teachers who care for children.

Characteristics and Abilities Needed
- Love, care for, and respect children.
- Have faith in God and the ability to share it.
- Have insight and understanding of how children learn and grow.
- Be willing work with others in ministry.
- Be willing to give of yourself and your time.
- Keep an open mind and willingness to risk and learn!

Training Opportunities
- Read periodicals and newsletters, such as *Forecast, Interpreter, iTeach,* and new materials in the field of children's ministry.
- Contact the appropriate annual conference and district staff to introduce yourself and communicate your congregation's needs for training; request new videos, books, and other resources / information from the conference center. Ask to have your name added to appropriate list serves and mailing lists.

- Participate in continuing education in district, conference, or ecumenical settings.
- Network with other area Christian educators and advocates of children.
- Attend FOCUS '09 or '13, a national United Methodist Conference for workers with children.
- Find or start a support group of children's coordinators in the area.

Accountability: Report or Relate to
- the pastor or church staff related to children's ministry
- the church council
- the nurture committee/ work area on education
- the staff/pastor-parish relations committee.

Term of Position: One year; may be renewed or renegotiated.

Time Requirements
- Be in attendance or available for Sunday mornings and weekday programming times.
- Communicate regularly with administrative groups.
- Communicate with teachers and parents regularly.
- Allow ample planning and study time.

Keeping Our Commitments to Children
The United Methodist Church

The primary task of The United Methodist Church is to make *faithful disciples of Jesus Christ,* including children, *for the transformation of the world.* You, too, are the church. Your primary task as a leader of children's ministries is to help the children in your congregation and community to be faithful disciples of Jesus Christ. That should be the foundation on which everything you do is built.

Paragraph 256.1 of the *Book of Discipline* states that in each local church there shall be a church school for the purpose of accomplishing the church's educational ministry. *It is not an option.* There is a continuing need to educate children. You were elected to serve as the leader in children's ministry for your congregation for a term of one year. You are called upon to fulfill the task set out in the *Discipline*. Keep in mind both what is said specifically about the coordinator and also what is included about Christian education, since both help to formulate comprehensive ministries with children.

In addition to the *Book of Discipline, The Book of Resolutions of The United Methodist Church* is an official document of the Church. Three resolutions are specifically of benefit to persons active in children's ministries: "Putting Children and Their Families First," "Reducing the Risk of Child Sexual Abuse in the Church," and "Childcare and the Church." Your pastor, church library, or district library may have a reference copy you can borrow to become familiar with these resolutions. You can purchase a copy from Cokesbury, www.cokesbury.com.

The general boards and agencies of The United Methodist Church take seriously the role of children in the congregation. The General Board of Discipleship, through the Office of Children's Ministries, provides resources for you and others working with children in local congregations. This includes national training events like FOCUS (a quadrennial conference for those who work in ministries with children planned for 2009 and 2013). This board also carries responsibility through the Curriculum Resource Committee and by working with The United Methodist Publishing House for developing the curriculum component for children. The General Board of Global Ministries advocates for children worldwide and supports United Methodist Women in their "Campaign for Children." The General Board of Church and Society advocates for children in legislative issues. The Commission on United

Methodist Men supports the office of Civic Youth Agencies/Scouting. Each of these boards employs staff persons whose major focus is for children. The General Commission on Finance and Administration provides support for congregations in matters of risk and in keeping children safe. Addresses and websites are available in Resources or by contacting your pastor.

Your annual conference has persons who care about children's ministries. Generally, conferences have a children's council, a coordinator of children's ministries, and/or a conference staff person responsible for children's ministries. Districts also may have persons in complementary positions. These people can help you know about district and conference programs and support for those who work with children. Some conferences have a chapter of Christian Educators Fellowship, whose members will share their knowledge and skills in ministry with children. You may wish to consider joining CEF (see Resources). Contact your conference office for information. Check with your church office or your pastor for the address and telephone number.

A Personal Commitment

As a young newlywed having recently moved to a new community, I visited the local United Methodist church. Within a few Sundays, I was invited to join the choir and later to help for one Sunday in the third- and fourth-grade Sunday school class. It wasn't long before I was teaching in vacation Bible school and Sunday school. I fell in love with helping children learn about God's love. That was more than thirty-five years ago, and I still have that same sensation of pure pleasure when working with children and, now, with adults who work with children. God draws me continually to new places, always with children as the focus. The blessings are many! Answer the following questions for yourself to help you prepare for your ministry.

What is your story? What circumstances brought you into children's ministry? Whom did God place in your life to encourage you? What event was the catalyst? Write your own story of how you came to this place of leadership in children's ministry. Tell why!

What special abilities and gifts has God given you? Some are teachers. Some are motivators. Some have gifts of planning or recruiting or visioning or creative problem solving or making terrific bulletin boards or instilling trust, or.... What gifts has God given to you? List the gifts you bring. After you have made your list, you may want to ask others what gifts they recognize in you that you may not have yet identified.

At different times in our lives, God speaks to us and leads us in new directions. At this time in your life, God has led you to be a blessing to children, to provide a foundation for their faith development, and to make the church a caring place to grow in God's love. **What is God saying to you now? What is your role at this time and in this place?**

How will your prayer life help you? Regardless of any other spiritual gift or Christian practice, be sure to support yourself and the children in your care with prayer. Even if a prayer is not answered in the way or time frame you desire, the act of prayer itself keeps your concern and your relationships with God and the children in the forefront of your mind and heart. For starters, use the prayer below or write your own.

A PRAYER FOR YOU
(Hint: This prayer may be used with the children's council by substituting plural pronouns for the singular.)

Almighty God, be with me. I come with a willing heart and many gifts to provide a safe and caring place in the church so that all children will grow in knowledge of you, commitment to Jesus Christ, and love for their neighbor. I ask that you grant the wisdom and vision necessary for the foundation of faith to undergird the children of this congregation. You sent Christ as the example of unconditional love. You sent the Holy Spirit to sustain us in times of difficulty and joy. Send me now to be a strong voice for children. Be with me so that the children of this congregation and community will know your kingdom. In Christ's name, I pray. Amen.

The Congregation's Commitment

In United Methodist churches, parents bring infants and very young children to be baptized. Parents promise to raise them in the Christian life. The congregation makes a commitment to "surround *these persons* with a community of love and forgiveness, that they may grow in *their* service to others" and to "pray for *them* that *they* may be true *disciples* who *walk* in the way that leads to life" (*The United Methodist Hymnal,* Baptismal Covenant II, page 40).

Children become a part of the church family and experience ministry in a variety of ways at an early age. Prayer in the home, at meals or bedtime, helps nurture them in the faith. They come to church and begin to experience the church as a "special place." They begin to interact with one another and learn about treating others with love and respect. As they grow older and become involved in ministry themselves, they begin to live out the promises made by their parents and the congregation at their baptism.

The ministry of Christian education is an all-encompassing task. In its broadest sense, it deals with every aspect of our lives. The Christian faith is communicated to children in essentially two places: the church and the family. It is the primary task of the church to transform persons into disciples. We help children grow in their faith in ways that are appropriate for their age level. They learn in many ways about how God is present in their lives. They participate in the life of the church through Sunday school, weekday settings, corporate worship, and acts of mission and service. At home, children see faith modeled by their parents, and they learn firsthand how to live as disciples.

QUESTIONS TO ASK.
Think about your congregation. What are the ways your congregation supports children and their families on their faith journey? What are your congregation's traditions for children's ministry? What vision does your congregation have for children's ministries? How are stories of the faith shared? What opportunities are available for children to express their faith through acts of service and leadership? How are parents sustained in the support of their children's Christian growth in the home? How are families supported in living out their faith when not at church? How are children helped to cope and heal after experiencing a crisis? How does your church support children in families headed by foster parents, grandparents who are raising grandchildren, single parents, same-sex parents, and incarcerated parents?

On a separate sheet of paper, develop a form similar to the one on page 18. (This chart is also available on the CD-ROM that accompanies the complete set of Guidelines.) Elicit help from other persons to complete it. This will help form a basis for your ministry with children.

Current Picture of Children's Ministry at _____ United Methodist Church

Children's Ministry Profile

Events/Program Ministries in Which Children Participate	Age of Persons Involved	Who Is Responsible? (Person and/or Group)	Budget Information, or How Does Funding Occur?	Values for Children	Values for Our Congregation
Sample: Vacation Bible School	3-yr-olds through 8th grades and their parents; childcare for younger children.	Education Committee + Lue, Kim & Maria, VBS Coordinators	Budget line items for Supplies, Equipment, Curriculum, etc.; Special donations are requested. No limit.	Stories of faith; Mission education; Fellowship; leading in worship; Fun; Shared experiences with parents; Developing relationships with others.	Opportunities for many adults to share faith with children. Outreach to community; Responding to needs for family involvement. Developing relationships with others.

18 GUIDELINES FOR LEADING YOUR CONGREGATION

What Is Your Role in Keeping Children Safe?

Sadly, the safety of children in the church and at church-sponsored events is no longer something to be taken for granted, as the tragic news from various religious settings has confirmed in recent years. *It is absolutely essential that the church have updated policies, procedures, and insurance coverage.*

If your congregation already has a child protection policy and procedures, then your role is assessment and advocacy.
- Become familiar with the protection policy and procedures that relate to children.
- Ensure that the policy and procedures are being followed in every dimension of your congregation's ministry with children.
- Take responsibility for yearly updating of procedures.
- Plan for regular communication with the congregation, teachers, parents. and staff regarding the procedures.
- Ask for time at staff meeting and church council to talk about the procedures three or four times a year or as often as seems appropriate in your congregation.
- Assess communication links with new members and new parents (such as the New Member Packet, Welcome to Our Church orientation event, Nursery Home Visitor packet, and so forth). Are your policies and procedures included?

If your congregation has no child protection policy and procedures, then your role is leadership.
- Get and read *Safe Sanctuaries: Reducing the Risk of Child Abuse in the Church,* available from Cokesbury (see Resources). This book will help your congregation work step-by-step to make your church a safer place for children and youth and for the adults who work with them.
- Involve other people, including the pastor, Christian educator, Education/Nurture Committee Chairperson, parents, trustees, and weekday ministry leaders.
- Request that the church council appoint a task force to study the issue and to bring a policy recommendation for formal church approval.
- Follow the steps outlined in *Safe Sanctuaries*.
- Call your conference office for support and training.

Children in the Life of the Congregation

> *At that time the disciples came to Jesus and asked, "Who is the greatest in the kingdom of heaven?" He called a child, whom he put among them, and said, "Truly I tell you, unless you change and become like children, you will never enter the kingdom of heaven. Whoever becomes humble like this child is the greatest in the kingdom of heaven. Whoever welcomes one such child in my name welcomes me.*
>
> *If any of you put a stumbling block before one of these little ones who believe in me, it would be better for you if a great millstone were fastened around your neck and you were drowned in the depth of the sea. Woe to the world because of stumbling blocks! Occasions for stumbling are bound to come, but woe to the one by whom the stumbling block comes!" (Matthew 18:1-7).*

Jesus was very clear: *Do not put stumbling blocks in the way of children!* Do we do that in the church? That certainly is not our intent, yet, sometimes we do.
- God gave children minds to think, but do we pay attention to their thoughts?
- God gave children bodies to move, but do we expect them to sit quietly in worship and not disturb the adults?
- God gave children a spirit, but do we fail to provide opportunities for them to express what is on their hearts?
- God gave children insight and abilities to care for others, but do we fail to provide opportunities for them to share their gift of caring with others?

In what ways does your church create stumbling blocks? (Create your list.)
-
-
-

In what ways does your church remove stumbling blocks and create a clear path for children to walk with God? (Create another list.)
-
-
-
-
-
-
-

Gifts Children Bring to the Church

Children have much to bring to the congregation. Children bring:
- a special spontaneity within congregational life that keeps us smiling, demands flexibility from us, and adds spice to our life together.
- the ability to see things as they really are.
- total-body worship of God.
- freshness in hymn singing, in celebrating God's love.
- new understanding of the world as seen through their eyes.
- a reminder of our own vows as we witness their baptism.
- their own confusion, isolation, discouragement, fears, loneliness, and pain.
- a filling of a void for persons who are childless, whose children are grown, or whose grandchildren live far away.
- the ability to make us shed tears because of their vulnerability.
- an unhesitating faith and absolute acceptance of God's love.
- questions that we forget to ask or are afraid to ask, that push us to think about our own theology, and that press us to articulate our beliefs in new ways. (Children keep us honest.)
- an openness to God.
- the ability to unlock love with a simple look.
- a way to connect us to today's real world.
- a challenge to an "old" way, consideration of a "new" way.
- pure, unadulterated JOY!

Children are God's unique gift to us. Do we have the awareness to accept and embrace the gift?

The Organizational Structure of the Church

because of your responsibility with children, you may have membership in a variety of different committees, councils, and/or task groups. Membership in these groups may seem to demand an overwhelming number of meetings. However, you may not need to be present at every one. Ask your pastor or staff person with whom you relate to help you complete the Congregational Meeting Commitment Worksheet in order to know what is expected of you. Remember: *Someone* should represent concerns of children when events are planned or when decisions are made. Your advocacy is important! Even in a very small congregation, it is important to have an advocate for children. That is you! Or maybe it is someone else you recruit. Fulfill your role with wisdom and caring.

Here are a few of the different groups you may be asked (or expected) to join:
- church council—the policy-making and decision-making body for the church.
- the nurture committee or commission on education work area (in many congregations the education work area relies on the coordinator of children's ministries to help plan for the needs of children). It is also important to have persons on the outreach and witness committees who have a heart for children.
- the council on children's ministries, which has responsibility, under the leadership of the coordinator of children's ministries (that may be you), for planning and overseeing the entire plan for ministry with children. (Although this is optional, it is particularly helpful. Information about organizing a Council on Children's Ministries can be found on page 24 of this Guideline.)
- the weekday ministries board. (In many congregations the coordinator of children's ministries may serve on the board of the weekday ministries program.)

Use the form on the next page to help organize your meeting schedule and commitments. Knowing who supports whom and who works with whom will help you determine which groups and meetings to relate to. One way your children's ministry fits into your church governance structure may be:

      Church council
          Nurture Committee
              Education Committee
                 Children's Council

Congregational Meeting Commitment Worksheet

Name of Group	Yes, I attend	No, I do not attend	Meeting Schedule	Written Reports	Oral Reports	My Leadership Role
Church Council						
Council on Children's Ministries						
Work Area on Education / Nurture Committee						
Weekday Ministries Board						

A Children's Ministries Council

Depending on the size of your church and the number of children you serve, there may be a need for a Children's Council. Consider forming such a council if your church has *any* of the following characteristics:
- a desire to create a shared ministry with parents, teachers, and congregation
- a large number of children
- two or more classes for each age level (preschool and elementary)
- many weekday activities
- full-day childcare or after-school care for school-age children
- many teachers.

A children's council may help to:
- study the needs of children
- ensure the safety of children involved in the congregation's ministries
- think through and plan possible program ministries with children
- talk and work with children and parents or other interested adults
- serve as the planning and implementing team for special children's projects and programs
- identify those with gifts for working with children and invite them to serve
- address the needs of special children
- write, revise, implement, and track policies that influence children's ministries.

The membership of the children's council, except for ex officio members, shall be selected by the committee on lay leadership and may include: representative teachers and leaders of children's activities of the church (including music and the other arts); representative parents; and representatives of work areas or committees (outreach, education, evangelism, missions, stewardship, and worship) related to the church's ministry with children. Ex officio members may include appropriate staff, the chairperson of the education or nurture committees, and the director of the church-sponsored weekday preschool or day care center. Membership should be set on a rotating basis similar to the process used with other committees in the congregation.

If your church does not have a children's council, begin to form one by:
- talking with your pastor
- getting approval from church council
- recruiting a task group to help with the formation
- developing written guidelines for the council
- celebrating the formation of the council.

Ministry for, with, and by Children

Think about all the ministry programs and opportunities available for the children of your church and community. Evaluate the variety of opportunities available for children in your congregation. *What is missing? What needs to be strengthened? What needs to change in content or format?* Look at how your congregation reaches out to receive all children, helps children relate their lives to God through Jesus Christ, helps children grow in Christian faith, and sends the children into their world to do God's work. Then ask: Do children have opportunities to:
- practice spiritual habits, such as prayer, worship attendance, and service to others
- learn and experience the biblical stories and music of the faith
- share their faith stories
- meet faith "saints" (people with a mature faith who are good examples for children and adults alike) in your own congregation
- experience Scripture at an appropriate developmental level
- learn "rituals" of the faith, such as "Jesus Loves Me," the Lord's Prayer, grace at mealtime, and the Doxology
- experience positive fellowship with other Christians—adults, youth, and children
- experience God's loving care through their teachers and group leaders
- experience opportunities to grow spiritually, physically, socially, psychologically, and emotionally in ways that are appropriate for their developmental level
- contribute to the life of the congregation
- be involved in mission education and stewardship education?

Following is a checklist prepared to show you possible patterns of children's ministry. *No congregation is expected to have every program imaginable. However, every congregation is expected to meet the faith needs of the children.* Use this list as a way to begin thinking about possibilities and standards for your congregation's ministry with children.

Develop your own list that fits the needs and the setting of your congregation. Think holistically. *Remember, the primary task is to help children to know God and to become faithful disciples of Jesus Christ.* This goal should undergird every option and should be the focus of every intersection of a child's life with the life of the congregation. Only *your congregation* knows the needs and possibilities of *your* setting.

CONGREGATIONAL OPPORTUNITIES FOR CHILDREN

A. Infants, toddlers, and twos are offered:
____ 1. love and acceptance as children of God
____ 2. clean rooms
____ 3. safe rooms
____ 4. clean and safe equipment, furniture, and toys
____ 5. trained, caring teachers
____ 6. Sunday school classes
____ 7. childcare when their parents are involved in church programs
____ 8. a nursery home visitor who connects with them and their parents regularly
____ 9. daycare throughout the week and/or Parent's Day or Morning Out programs
____10. food, clothing, and shelter as needed
____11. a welcome place in worship, fellowship events, and other events where the church family comes together
____12. the opportunity for continuing and dynamic faith development.

B. Preschool Children (ages 3, 4, and 5) are offered:
____ 1. love and acceptance as children of God
____ 2. safe rooms that fit their size, interests, and abilities
____ 3. opportunities for continuing and dynamic faith development
____ 4. Sunday school classes and other discipleship learning opportunities
____ 5. vacation Bible school classes
____ 6. music experiences through Sunday school and/or a children's choir
____ 7. opportunities to be involved in the stewardship program of the church
____ 8. trained, caring teachers
____ 9. adult friends with whom they feel comfortable
____10. mission studies and opportunities for involvement in mission projects
____11. food, clothing, or shelter as needed
____12. encouragement and support when they bring friends with them to church
____13. weekday classes, such as preschool, daycare, play groups, nursery school
____14. inclusion in corporate worship services of the congregation
____15. quality childcare when their parents are involved in church programs
____16. fellowship times at the church
____17. games, music, and creative activities.

C. Children in the elementary grades are offered:
____ 1. love and acceptance as children of God
____ 2. safe rooms that fit their size, interest, and abilities
____ 3. opportunities for continuing and dynamic faith development
____ 4. Sunday school classes and other discipleship learning opportunities
____ 5. trained, caring teachers and comfortable adult friends
____ 6. opportunities for mission studies, mission projects, justice issues
____ 7. opportunity for stewardship activities and projects
____ 8. vacation Bible school and/or special summer programs
____ 9. after-school care while parents are still at work
____10. fellowship experiences
____11. choir and other music opportunities
____12. Girl and Boy Scout programs, Camp Fire, 4-H groups
____13. opportunities to serve in worship through litanies, prayers, Scripture reading, ushering, and acolyting
____14. concurrent, appropriate programs when parents are involved in adult church programs
____15. food, clothing, or shelter as needed
____16. encouragement to bring friends to church activities
____17. support groups for special concerns such as, divorce of parents, death or other significant loss, and serious illness of sibling
____18. opportunities for intergenerational relationships.

D. Parents of children are offered:
____ 1. opportunities for continuing and dynamic faith development
____ 2. parenting classes
____ 3. Sunday school classes of interest to them
____ 4. food, clothing, shelter as needed
____ 5. assurance of a safe place for their children
____ 6. support groups for special concerns such as loss of a child or spouse, child abuse, substance abuse, or divorce
____ 7. support from the pastor, professional educator, and church staff
____ 8. opportunities to learn about baptism, Communion, and worship
____ 9. knowledge of what their children are studying
____10. opportunities to teach or lead children's groups
____11. resources to learn the ways children grow and what children need
____12. knowledge of what is happening in the community that affects children and the role of the church in the community
____13. knowledge about opportunities to act in support of children in their own communities and throughout the world.

(This chart is available on the CD-ROM that accompanies the complete set of Guidelines.)

Ministry in the Community and the World

Children can and should take an active part in mission and stewardship activities in their church, community, and world.

Children, especially middle and older elementary children, are interested in and aware of the needs of others. This is a wonderful time to expand their horizons beyond the local church to the community and world around them. They also have an interest in fairness. Combine these two age-level characteristics and you have fertile ground for an extended ministry in several areas. *Sprouts* (see Resources) is an excellent source that provides ways to help children develop habits of spirituality and action.

MISSION AND STEWARDSHIP

The development of good habits of giving and mission work can't wait until children grow to be adults. Introduce children to mission and stewardship issues. Offer a variety of experiences and opportunities for children and their parents (and for the whole congregation) that provide information as well as possibilities to practice giving for others.

Each year the General Board of Discipleship makes available program packets for "The United Methodist Children's Fund for Christian Mission." These packets are free to your church. They describe specific children's mission projects in the United States and around the world. Children are invited to undertake projects in which they learn more about children in specific locations and about mission in general.

All children can become aware of the needs of their communities and the world through such projects as UNICEF, CROP walks, and Heifer Project International. Hold events such as mission fairs, mission Sundays, special project Sundays, and mission summer camp. Select a kit (school, health, sewing, cleaning, layette) for children to build for UMCOR. Set aside some time for children to experience the mission study of a country while United Methodist Women are involved in the study. Consider "Hope for the Children of Africa" or "Nothing But Nets" as a special mission project.

Include children in stewardship education events and in churchwide stewardship projects. There are many age-appropriate ways for children to understand the stewardship of prayers, presence, gifts, and service. "Let the Children Give" is an excellent print resource. "Stewardship Nuggets" (www.gbod.org/stewardship/articles) helps parents guide children toward a faith-grounded relationship with money, giving, and stewardship.

There are agencies both within the local community and within The United Methodist Church that can help you plan projects and provide information to increase awareness of mission arenas. Contact the persons in your church, district, or conference who serve in the areas of mission and stewardship. Ask for help and information about the possibilities for including children in the extended mission of your church.

CAMPING

Every conference provides a variety of camping opportunities for children. Church camps provide age-appropriate faith experiences that frequently lead to a life-changing commitment to God. They also provide a place to bond with other United Methodist children and to pursue special interest areas. Other camping opportunities are available through your congregation's participation in Girl Scouts, Boy Scouts, Camp Fire, and 4-H programs. Lifelong friendships often begin in children's camping experiences. In these settings, children are nurtured in a totally different environment. Provide publicity well in advance, as well as funding and transportation for children to attend conference church camp.

REACHING OUT TO THE COMMUNITY

Invite children from the community to your existing programs and ministries. Be alert in your church community to discover some of the needs of children. Is your church located in an area where an after-school program is needed? Perhaps daycare or ill-child care for working parents might be a blessing to your community. What about a tutoring program to meet the educational needs of children? Are there children who are hungry or in need of clothing? You, as coordinator of children's ministries, have a multitude of opportunities to expand the ministries of your church to meet the needs of local children. You can help to create a winning situation for everyone. The neighborhood elementary school(s) will be helpful in an identification process.

When forming or growing a ministry that reaches out and draws in children and families from the community, expect the possibility that congregation members may not be prepared. Provide a continuing educational component for the congregation that includes a biblical mandate, theological understandings, faith dimensions, and practical examples.

INCLUSIVENESS AND ECUMENICAL AWARENESS

Jesus said, "Go forth into all the world." That commission is not limited to those who are in our country, or look like us, or speak the same language, or celebrate like we do. There are many opportunities for children to learn about others who are different from themselves—whether it is in terms of race, ethnicity, economics, physical or mental ability, or religious beliefs. Be deliberate about providing opportunities for children to learn about and to appreciate others. Provide anti-bias training for adults who work with children. Make discoveries about other religious programs; share ideas, and learn from and about one another. You might invite children from a synagogue or mosque to share their traditions and beliefs (after appropriate preparation for all involved.) World Communion Sunday (the first Sunday of October) is a natural time to learn about other Christian denominations around the world. Join with other congregations near you in a neighborhood vacation Bible school, Thanksgiving program, or Children's Sabbath observance.

CHILDREN'S SABBATH
Each year people of faith gather in churches, synagogues, temples, and other houses of faith to lift up the needs of children. Become a part of this special weekend of learning, praying, advocacy, and worship. Contact the Children's Defense Fund (see Resources) for a Children's Sabbath planning guide. Invite other congregations and faiths to join the planning. The third weekend of October has been chosen by CDF and the second weekend in October was selected by General Conference of The United Methodist Church. If either of these will not work for your congregation, select another time.

PRESERVING CREATION
The important issues of ecology and environment, centering on stewardship of our Earth home, present excellent arenas in which children may become actively involved. Recycling and area cleanup projects provide fun learning (and productive) experiences for children of all ages. These can be organized with adult groups in your congregation, as a fellowship group or after-school program, or with a Sprouts program.

Organize and Plan for the Year

Check and double-check your plans to ensure a smooth-running program. Some churches provide programming the year round; others, from September through June. *No matter what pattern your church follows, a year-long planning calendar is a must.*

Find out where your complete church calendar is kept, who records information, and how to schedule the events for which you are responsible. Note those events already on the church calendar that include or affect children's ministries. It is also helpful to be aware of community events. Get a calendar like The United Methodist Program Calendar (see Resources), which includes planning suggestions. Begin with those dates already set on your church calendar. To avoid conflicts, list upcoming dates of events planned for children and coordinate programming with other church ministries. Meet regularly with staff to look ahead at upcoming events.

List meetings and events that are already set. Block time to prepare for quality programming. Add to these activities the dates for ordering curriculum: July, October, January, April (or when appropriate for your curriculum). Also, note dates for purchasing attendance books and supplies. Call your conference and district offices to find out dates for teacher training events and church camp experiences. Setting up the calendar is critical to your program ministries.

Now, take a look at what is planned. Are there opportunities to help children grow as disciples and as spiritual beings? Is there a variety of activities for children's varying interests? Are family and intergenerational experiences included? What is missing? Where are potential difficulties? What will take long-term planning or group planning? For additional help in planning, see chapter 3 of *The Ministry of Christian Education and Formation: A Practical Guide for your Congregation* (see Resources).

As the coordinator of children's ministries you are a link in the connectional system of The United Methodist Church. Through you, in cooperation with the work area or committee chairpersons, the resources and experiences of the denomination become available to your local church. Call upon the services and resources of the district and conference coordinators of children's ministries. Pastors and district superintendents can furnish names and addresses of these persons for you. Plan to attend FOCUS, (see page 14). Budget for this in advance. Check with district and conference personnel about upcoming events for workers with children, and see the inside back cover for general agency contacts.

Weekday Ministries

Weekday ministry is possible in any size church. In all churches, the goal and the vision must be that which is best for children. In 2008, General Conference revised a resolution on "Child Care and the Church." This resolution guides a congregation's ministry through the week with children to assure that quality programs are established and implemented to meet the physical, emotional, spiritual, and mental needs of children today. Jesus said, "Let the little children come to me" (Mark 10:14). He also said, "Whoever welcomes one such child in my name welcomes me" (Matthew 18:5).

Childcare in the church is not a new field. Several thousand of our congregations sponsor weekday programs such as daycare; Parents' Day Out; preschool; after-school care; and respite care for children with handicapping, abusive, or other special conditions. Many of these programs are intentional ministries of the congregations. Some are integrated holistically as a congregational ministry and some use space rented from a church.

We can fully accept children as Jesus did. We can invite them into our fellowship and nurture them.

What Is Weekday Ministry?

Weekday ministry is *mission* work at its very best. The most important resource of any society is its children. Many children in our communities are in need of safe, quality care during times when parents are at work.

Weekday ministry is Christian education, nurture, and faith development. During the critical early childhood and early elementary years, children form basic attitudes about the world and themselves. It is during this time that children form trust, the fundamental requirement for faith development. The church best reflects the Christian faith when it supports families at this crucial time and provides an example of the highest, Christlike qualities.

Weekday ministry is stewardship. Rooms that might otherwise be empty throughout the week are used for the education and formation of children.

Weekday ministry is evangelism. Families of young children who have found love and concern for their children in your church's weekday ministry often become part of the church family. Regardless of whether this happens, people are still receiving the good news of God's love through interactions with people of faith.

Weekday ministry is a business requiring dependable income, realistic expense projections, binding agreements, accountability, and liability.

WHAT WEEKDAY MINISTRY IS NOT
It is also important to note what weekday ministry is not.

Weekday ministry is *not* a fundraiser. Everything has a price tag. Depending on the form of your program, participants expect to be charged appropriate tuition and fees, which include the expenses for utilities, supplies, and teachers. Tuition will not affect the tax-exempt status of the church if your church is incorporated and your policy statement shows the relationship of the weekday program to the governing body of the church. Although fees may cover the expenses of the program, quality care is expensive. Your church should not expect to make money from any weekday ministry. Any excess funds should be held in trust for "lean" times in the ministry and for increasing benefits for staff in a field that is generally underpaid.

Weekday ministry is not easy. Weekday ministry means shared space. It means wear and tear on the building, more things to store, and more programs to schedule. Meeting licensing requirements may require installation of smoke detectors or push-bar doors. In regions where it snows, the parking lot has to be plowed on days other than Sunday. Other requirements may include regular testing of the water supply, the fire extinguishers, and the safety of the building to meet health department codes. Meeting the requirements will provide a safer place for all persons for every day of the week. Whether or not there is a weekday ministry, most of these requirements should be in effect for the safety of all persons in your building.

ACCOUNTABILITY
All education in a United Methodist church is provided through the nurture or education committees. A weekday ministry board would work with and report to the committee or group responsible for Christian education in the church. The staff/pastor-parish relations committee might be responsible (with the weekday ministry board) in hiring the director.

RESPONSIBILITY
A weekday program cannot be taken lightly or casually. It is a sacred trust and a legal and moral responsibility. Once begun, it needs perpetual care and nurturing. The congregation needs to assess its understanding of discipleship as it relates to the weekday ministry program and to reassess and update the program periodically. The Resources section suggests guides for beginning or reevaluating a program.

Weekday Ministry Programs

WHAT ABOUT WEEKDAY MINISTRY PROGRAMS?
Regardless of the kinds of weekday ministry offered, the church has an opportunity and the mandate to include children from various socioeconomic, cultural, and racial and ethnic backgrounds. Children learn by example. They first develop faith through trust in the adults around them. Their parents often select church-based weekday programs because they feel they can trust the church to care for their children regardless of their own religious affiliation or background. We must work hard to keep that trust by providing quality learning experiences in a safe environment.

A weekday ministry board may be responsible for governing one or more of the following programs in your church. For assistance in setting up or training a weekday ministry board, see the *Director's Manual for Weekday Ministry* (see Resources).

FOR YOUNGER CHILDREN (INFANTS THROUGH KINDERGARTEN)
Daycare: A program for infants, toddlers, and pre-elementary children that may begin as early as 7:00 A.M. or earlier and continue as late as 6:00 P.M. or later. It provides care and meals and offers developmentally appropriate activities in a safe atmosphere of love and concern for each child.

Preschool/Nursery School: A half-day program for children two to five years old that provides developmentally sound activities in an atmosphere of love and concern for each child. Sometimes this may include prekindergarten.

Kindergarten: Generally a full-day program for children five years of age that has the added goals of teaching readiness skills to children prior to entrance into first grade.

Parents' Day/Night Out Program: A half-day, all-day, or evening program of care and activities for children while parents are provided free time.

Play Day: A regular or occasional day for young children to gather with their parents for play. This is a time for parents to interact while their children play safely with them in the church nursery, on the church playground, or at a park.

Care for Special Needs Children: A program for children who are recovering from physical or emotional trauma or abuse, with autism, for whom

English is a second language and who need tutoring, or who have other special needs. Establishing such a program could provide a service that is unavailable in the community.

FOR OLDER CHILDREN

Before- and After-School Care: A program that provides a safe and enriching atmosphere for school-age children who otherwise would be without supervision before and after school. The program could be extended to a full-time program during the summer or school holidays. Activities may include faith enrichment fellowship, clubs, scouting groups, music, service projects, and academic enrichment.

Fellowship Groups: Meet once a week or less. They provide opportunities for children to learn and have fun within the church. These groups frequently provide preparation for entry into the church's youth group.

Telephone Ministry to "Latchkey" Children: A program in which children could call or be called when they are alone at home. It is an excellent way to connect children with caring adults.

FOR ALL CHILDREN

Ill-Child Care: A specialized ministry for children who have minor illnesses, such as colds or flu. Working parents are especially grateful for this ministry.

Evening/Night Care: A full-time program is particularly important for parents who work second or third shifts.

Resources

** Denotes our top picks

- *Campaign for Children—Phase III,* 1-800-305-9857. Special emphasis of United Methodist Women.

- *Children's Sabbath* Yearly planning manual available from Children's Defense Fund. (See Resource Agencies on page 38.)

- ***Children Worship!* by MaryJane Pierce Norton (Nashville: Discipleship Resources, 1997. ISBN 978-0-88177-223-4). Thirteen-session worship education resource helps congregations incorporate children (ages 5–8) into the worshiping community. Can easily be adapted for parenting classes and intergenerational retreats.

- ***The Children's Minister,* by Rita B. Hays (Nashville: Discipleship Resources, 2007. ISBN 978-0-88177-527-3). This book guides the reader to new understandings of how to be a pastor to children when the times are tough, as well as in the everyday life of the church family. A "must have" for every congregational leader in children's ministry.

- *Children's Ministry,* by Adam Hamilton and Judy Comstock (Nashville: Abingdon Press, 2007. ISBN 978-0-687-33413-1). Ideas for recruiting volunteers, screening and security, connecting with kids, and programs.

- *Community with Children and the Poor: A Guide for Congregational Study* by Debra Smith (Nashville: Cokesbury, 2003. ISBN X516543). A resource in support of the Bishops Initiative on Children and Poverty, relating beyond local settings to systemic and global issues.

- ***The First Three Years: A Guide for Ministry With Infants, Toddlers, and Two-Year-Olds,* by Mary Alice Donovan Gran, editor (Nashville: Discipleship Resources, 1995, 2001. ISBN 978-0-88177-324-8). A comprehensive manual for the congregation's ministry to young children and their families. Completely reproducible.

- *Foundations: Shaping the Ministry of Christian Education in Your Congregation* (Nashville: Discipleship Resources, 1993. ISBN 978-0-88177-123-7). Provides a foundation for building a solid Christian education ministry in your congregation.

- *iTeach.* Monthly free e-letter from the General Board of Discipleship. Subscribe at www.gbod.org/education.

- **The Ministry of Christian Education and Formation: A Practical Guide for Your Congregation,* by the Christian education staff of the General Board of Discipleship (GBOD) (Nashville: Discipleship Resources, 2003. ISBN 978-0-88177-395-8). A helpful and practical "must have" book for planning Christian education ministries for your congregation.

- *Pockets* magazine (Nashville: Upper Room). A devotional magazine with Bible study, games, activities, and stories specifically for school-aged children. Available by individual or group subscription.

- *Safe Sanctuaries: Reducing the Risk of Child Abuse in the Church,* by Joy Thornburg Melton (Nashville: Discipleship Resources, 1998. ISBN 978-0-88177-220-3). Outlines policies and procedures to help congregations be safe places for children and youth and for the adults who care for them.

- **Sprouts: Covenant Discipleship with Children,* by Edie Genung Harris and Shirley Ramsey (Nashville: Discipleship Resources, 2002. ISBN 978-0-88177-389-7). Explains weekly support for children grades 3-6 to live as disciples of Christ.

- *What Every Leader Needs to Know* [Series] (Nashville: Discipleship Resources, 2004).

- **Look for more teaching and teacher helps at www.gbod.org/education and at Sunday School: It's for life at www.sundayschool.cokesbury.com.

FROM THE OFFICE OF CHILDREN'S MINISTRY

The following four resources are available by download from the web site or by contacting The Office of Children's Ministries at the General Board of Discipleship (www.gbod.org/children); telephone 1-877-899-2780 Ext. 1761.

- **The United Methodist Children's Fund for Christian Mission.* A packet that includes a map and six annual projects for mission education for children.

- *"Childcare and the Church," The Book of Resolutions,* 2008. The official statement on weekday ministry of The United Methodist Church. (Check also with your pastor.)

- *Faith Development of Children.* A concise look at how children grow and develop. Includes a chart.

- *Information: Children's Ministries* newsletter. Back issues are available.

MISSION PROJECTS FOR CHILDREN

- **The United Methodist Children's Fund for Christian Mission, P.O. Box 340003, Nashville, TN 37203-0003. Phone 1-877-899-2780 Ext. 1761.

- Heifer Project International, 1 World Avenue, Little Rock, AR 72202. Phone 800-422-0474 or www.heifer.org.

- School or Health Kits, United Methodist Committee on Relief (UMCOR), UMCOR Depot, 101 Sager Brown Road, P.O. Box 850, Baldwin. LA 70514-0850. Phone 800-814-8765. www.sagerbrown.org.

- UNICEF, 3 United Nations Plaza, New York, NY 10017. Phone 212-326-7000 or www.unicef.org.

WEEKDAY MINISTRIES RESOURCES

- *Civic Youth Serving Agencies/Scouting Packet,* available free from Civic Youth Serving/Scouting Office of United Methodist Men. P.O. Box 340006, Nashville, TN 37203-0006; lcoppock@gcumm.org.

- *Director's Manual for Weekday Ministries,* by Barbara Snell McLain (Nashville, Discipleship Resources, 2003. ISBN 978-0-88177-383-5).

- *Wonder Filled Weekdays.* 65 lesson plans for teachers of preschoolers in Christian preschool ministries. Download from www.cokesbury.com.

RESOURCE AGENCIES

- *Children's Defense Fund.* Advocacy for children. Sponsors Children's Sabbath. Newsletter and other helpful information available about today's children. 25 E Street, NW. Washington, DC 20001. 202-628-8787 or www.childrensdefense.org.

- ***Christian Educators Fellowship.* Professional group for persons, both volunteer and employed, who are leading Christian educational ministries in congregations. CEF is a national organization that also has annual conference chapters. Contact Ellen Thompson, Christian Educators Fellowship Office, P.O. Box 24930, Nashville, TN 37202, 615-749-6870 or www.cefumc.org.

- *Cokesbury.* Provides children's curriculum resources that are endorsed by the Curriculum Resources Committee (CRC) for use in United

Methodist churches (check for the CRC symbol in catalogs). *Forecast* (curriculum catalog) and Curric-U-Phone staff (1-800-251-8591) can help with resource selection. Call 800-672-1789 or visit Cokesbury.com.

- *National AfterSchool Association.* Professional association for those in after school and summer care of school age children. 529 Main Street, Suite 214, Charlestown, MA 02129. 800-617-8242 or www.naaweb.org.

- *National Association for the Education of Young Children* (NAEYC). Accredits high quality early childhood programs. Its membership organization publishes the magazine Young Children, as well as books, pamphlets, videos, and posters. Write to NAEYC, 1313 L Street NW, Suite 500, Washington DC, 20005. Telephone 1-800-424-2460 or www.naeyc.org for membership information and resource list.

- *School Age Notes: Resources for AfterSchool Professionals.* Excellent newsletter resource for after-school and summertime weekday ministry for school-aged children. P.O. Box 476, New Albany, OH 43054, 800-410-8780 or www.schoolagenotes.com.

- *Department of Human Services.* Each state sets standards for preschool and school-aged programs. Contact your state office for the licensing standards. Additionally, school principals and counselors, community health personnel, scout leaders, and others are helpful connections in meeting the needs of all children in your community.

GENERAL CHURCH RESOURCES

- *The Book of Discipline of The United Methodist Church,* 2008 (Nashville: The United Methodist Publishing House; available from Cokesbury).

- *Guidelines for Leading Your Congregation: 2009–2012* (Nashville: Abingdon Press; available from Cokesbury). Especially appropriate Guidelines: Christian Education, Small Group Ministries, and Scouting and Civic Youth Serving Ministry.

- *Sharing God's Gifts* (United Methodist Communications, Free, Call 1-888-862-3242) About the structure and organization of The United Methodist Church.

- *Program Calendar* (United Methodist Communications, Call 1-888-862-3242). Available in a variety of formats. Contains various helps for planning for United Methodists congregations.